West Virginia

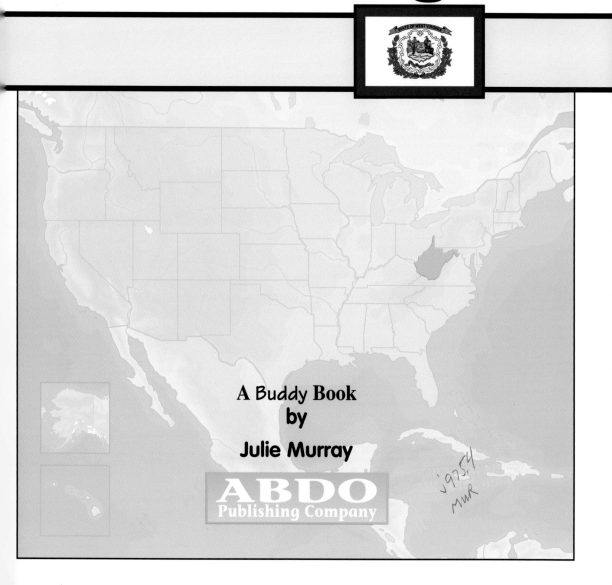

A Buddy Book
by
Julie Murray

ABDO
Publishing Company

VISIT US AT
www.abdopub.com

Published by ABDO Publishing Company, 4940 Viking Drive, Edina, Minnesota 55435.

Copyright © 2006 by Abdo Consulting Group, Inc. International copyrights reserved in all countries. No part of this book may be reproduced in any form without written permission from the publisher. Buddy Books™ is a trademark and logo of ABDO Publishing Company.

Printed in the United States.

Edited by: Sarah Tieck
Contributing Editor: Michael P. Goecke
Graphic Design: Deb Coldiron, Maria Hosley
Image Research: Sarah Tieck
Photographs: AP/Wide World, Clipart.com, Comstock, Corbis, Getty Images, Library of Congress, One Mile Up, Photodisc, Special Thanks to the National Scenic Byways Program (www.byways.com) for use of the photo on page 5

Library of Congress Cataloging-in-Publication Data

Murray, Julie, 1969-
    West Virginia / Julie Murray.
       p. cm. — (The United States)
    Includes index.
    Contents: A snapshot of West Virginia — Where is West Virginia? — All about West Virginia — Cities and the capital — Famous citizens — West Virginia's landscape — Coal mining — Monogahela National Forest — A history of West Virginia.
    ISBN 1-59197-707-X
       1. West Virginia—Juvenile literature. I. Title.

F241.3.M87 2005
975.4—dc22

2005048079

Table Of Contents

A Snapshot Of West Virginia

West Virginia is known for its history. One important part of this history is West Virginia's relationship with the state of Virginia. The state of West Virginia was part of Virginia until the American Civil War. When Virginia joined the Confederate States of America in 1861, many of the state's western counties stayed loyal to the Union. They formed their own government. In 1863, these counties became the state of West Virginia.

There are 50 states in the United States. Every state is different. Every state has an official nickname. West Virginia is nicknamed "The Mountain State." This nickname refers to the Appalachian Mountains, which run through the entire state.

West Virginia has many scenic roads such as this one.

West Virginia became the 35th state on June 20, 1863. It has 24,231 square miles (62,758 sq km) of land. It is the 41st-largest state in the United States. West Virginia is home to 1,808,344 people.

Mills such as this one are part of West Virginia's history.

Where Is West Virginia?

There are four parts of the United States. Each part is called a region. Each region is in a different area of the country. The United States Census Bureau says the four regions are the Northeast, the South, the Midwest, and the West.

West Virginia is located in the South region of the United States. West Virginia's weather is mild. Summers are hot and humid. Some parts of the state, such as the mountains, are cooler and can even get snow.

Four Regions of the United States of America

ALASKA

WASHINGTON

OREGON

IDAHO

MONTANA

WYOMING

NEVADA

UTAH

CALIFORNIA

ARIZONA

NEW MEXICO

COLORADO

NORTH DAKOTA

SOUTH DAKOTA

NEBRASKA

KANSAS

OKLAHOMA

TEXAS

MINNESOTA

IOWA

MISSOURI

ARKANSAS

LOUISIANA

WISCONSIN

MICHIGAN

ILLINOIS

INDIANA

OHIO

KENTUCKY

TENNESSEE

MISSISSIPPI

ALABAMA

GEORGIA

WEST VIRGINIA

VIRGINIA

NORTH CAROLINA

SOUTH CAROLINA

FLORIDA

VERMONT

MAINE

NEW HAMPSHIRE

MASSACHUSETTS

NEW YORK

RHODE ISLAND

CONNECTICUT

PENNSYLVANIA

NEW JERSEY

DELAWARE

Washington D.C.

MARYLAND

HAWAII

West

Midwest

South

Northeast

West Virginia is bordered by five other states. Pennsylvania and Maryland are northeast. Virginia is east and south. Kentucky is southwest. Ohio is northwest.

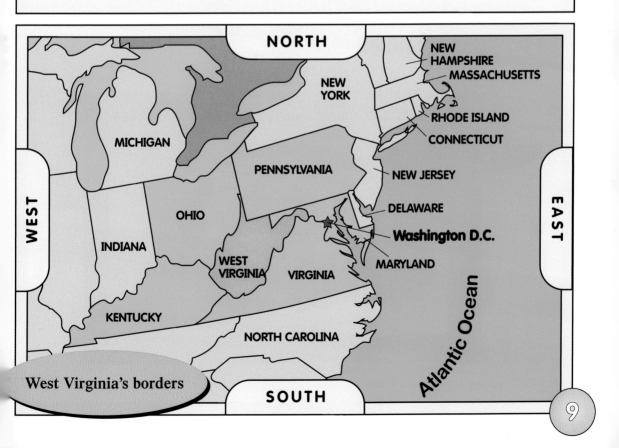

West Virginia's borders

West Virginia

State abbreviation: WV

State nickname: The Mountain State

State capital: Charleston

State motto: *Montani semper liberi* (Latin for "Mountaineers Are Always Free")

Statehood: June 20, 1863, 35th state

Population: 1,808,344, ranks 37th

State flag:
Adopted in 1929

Land area: 24,231 square miles (62,758 sq km), ranks 41st

State tree: Sugar maple

State song: "The West Virginia Hills"

State government: Three branches: legislative, executive, and judicial

Average July temperature: 72°F (22°C)

Average January temperature: 32°F (0°C)

State flower: Rhododendron

State animal: Black bear

State bird: Cardinal

Cities And The Capital

Charleston is the capital city of West Virginia. It is also the largest city in the state. The city is located along the banks of the Kanawha River. Charleston became the state capital in 1885. Before that, it was also the capital from 1870 to 1875. There is a golden dome on the capitol building.

Huntington is the second-largest city in West Virginia. It is located in the southwestern part of the state, along the Ohio River. The metropolitan area of Huntington extends into Kentucky and Ohio. Many products are manufactured in Huntington. The Ohio River is used for shipping.

West Virginia's State Capitol

Famous Citizens

Booker T. Washington (1856–1915)

Booker T. Washington was born in Virginia. He and his parents were slaves. When they were freed, they moved to Malden, West Virginia. Washington grew up to be a teacher. He is famous for helping to make things better for other African Americans.

He was the founder of what is now Tuskegee University in Tuskegee, Alabama. This was a school for African Americans.

Booker T. Washington

Famous Citizens

Pearl S. Buck (1892–1973)

Pearl S. Buck was born in Hillsboro in 1892. She grew up in China. She was famous for writing books. *The Good Earth* is one of her most famous novels. It is about a Chinese peasant. Buck received a Pulitzer Prize for this in 1932. In 1938, she received the Nobel Prize for Literature. These are important awards for writers.

Pearl S. Buck

Famous Citizens

Mary Lou Retton (1968–)

Mary Lou Retton was born in Fairmont in 1968. She is famous for being a gymnast. Retton won five medals at the 1984 Olympic games. She also won the women's Olympic All-Around Title. Today, she is still the only American to have won this.

Mary Lou Retton

Appalachian Mountains

The Appalachian Mountains run through the state of West Virginia. They are the second-largest mountain range in North America. They stretch for about 1,500 miles (2,414 km) from Quebec, Canada, to Birmingham, Alabama. The only mountain range in North America that is larger is the Rocky Mountains.

In West Virginia, the Allegheny Mountain range is part of the Appalachian Mountains. The highest point in the state is there. It is Spruce Knob, which stands 4,861 feet (1,482 m) high.

A view of Blackwater Canyon
in the Allegheny Mountains.

A view of the Blue Ridge Mountains.

The Blue Ridge Mountains are also part of the Appalachian Mountains. They run through the eastern part of West Virginia. Many of the state's farms and natural resources are in this area.

The trees turn colors during autumn in the mountains.

Coal

Coal is a dark-colored rock

Coal can be burned for fuel. Much of the electricity in the United States comes from coal.

Coal is one of West Virginia's largest natural resources. Deposits of coal can be found beneath more than half of the state's land.

People used to go into mines to get the coal. Coal mining was a dangerous job. The coal was deep in the ground. And, the ground could cave in. Also, the coal dust could make the miners sick. Today, machines do most of the work of coal mining.

People who worked in the mines were called miners.

Monongahela National Forest

Monongahela National Forest is located in eastern West Virginia. This area includes mountains, valleys, rivers, streams, and forests. Some say the name "Monongahela" comes from a Native American word. The word means "the river of falling banks."

There are a variety of activities to be enjoyed at Monongahela National Forest. People go there to hike, bike, camp, fish, and ride horses.

People go white-water rafting in Monongahela National Forest.

Seneca Rocks is a popular place for rock climbers. This rock formation is a famous landmark in West Virginia. It is located near the North Fork River in Monongahela National Forest.

A view of Seneca Rocks.

A rock climber scaling the side
of a rock formation.

West Virginia

1606: King James I of England gives the Virginia colony to a business group. This group is called the Virginia Group of London.

1727: A settlement is established at New Mecklenburg. Later, this area will be known as Shepherdstown.

1742: John P. Salling and John Howard discover coal in West Virginia.

1775: Natural gas is discovered. This happens near Charleston.

1836: The first railroad in West Virginia reaches Harpers Ferry.

1859: John Brown leads a raid at Harpers Ferry.

1863: The western part of Virginia becomes West Virginia. West Virginia becomes the 35th state on June 20.

1907: On December 6, two mines explode in Monongah. The blasts kill 362 people. This is the worst disaster ever in a United States mine.

1954: The West Virginia Turnpike connects the cities of Charleston and Princeton.

2003: Floodwaters cause major damage in southern West Virginia.

This home was damaged by floodwaters.

Cities in West Virginia

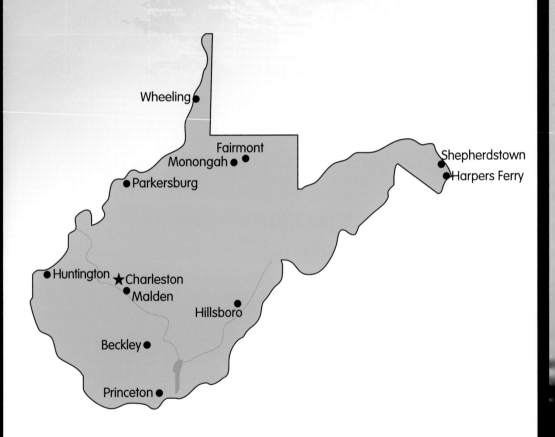

Wheeling ●

Fairmont
Monongah ● ● Fairmont

Shepherdstown ●
Harpers Ferry ●

Parkersburg ●

Huntington ● ★ Charleston
● Malden

Hillsboro ●

Beckley ●

Princeton ●

Important Words

American Civil War the United States war between the Northern and the Southern states.

capital a city where government leaders meet.

metropolitan a large city, usually with smaller cities called suburbs

mine a large hole made in the earth that people use to get a natural resource.

nickname a name that describes something special about a person or a place.

slave a person who is bought and sold as property.

Web Sites

To learn more about West Virginia, visit ABDO Publishing Company on the World Wide Web. Web site links about West Virginia are featured on our Book Links page. These links are routinely monitored and updated to provide the most current information available.

www.abdopub.com

Index